SHIT HERE
we go
AGAIN

SORRY
I CAN'T COME
IN TODAY,
I'M SICK OF
THAT
FUCKING
PLACE

THAT AIN'T
My fucking
PROBLEM

JUST DO
YOUR
GODDAMN
HOME
work

KISSMYASS

SCREW THIS i'm GOING home!

I GIVE JUST
enough
FUCKS TO
stay EMPL
OYeD

I'M LATE
Fucking
deal
WITH IT

IM NOT
doing
THAT SHIT

I DON'T NEED
ANGER
MANAGE
-MENT
I NEED PEOPLE
TO STOP
DOING STUPID
SHIT THAT
PISSES
ME
OFF!

I DON'T NEED TO CALM DOWN, I NEED PEOPLE TO STOP DOING STUPID SHIT

I HAVE
PLENTY OF
TALENT &
VISION
I JUST
DON't GIVE
A DAMN

HOW ABOUT
never
?
IS
NEVER
FUCKING
GOOD
FOR
YOU
?

how the
FUCK
is it
MONDAY

I DON'T
GET PAID
ENOUGH
FOR THIS
SHIT

DON'T
ASK me
TO DO
shit UNTIL
I'VE had
COFFEE

Fuck
THIS SHIT
o'clock

friday
IS
MY SECOND
FAVORITE
F-WORD

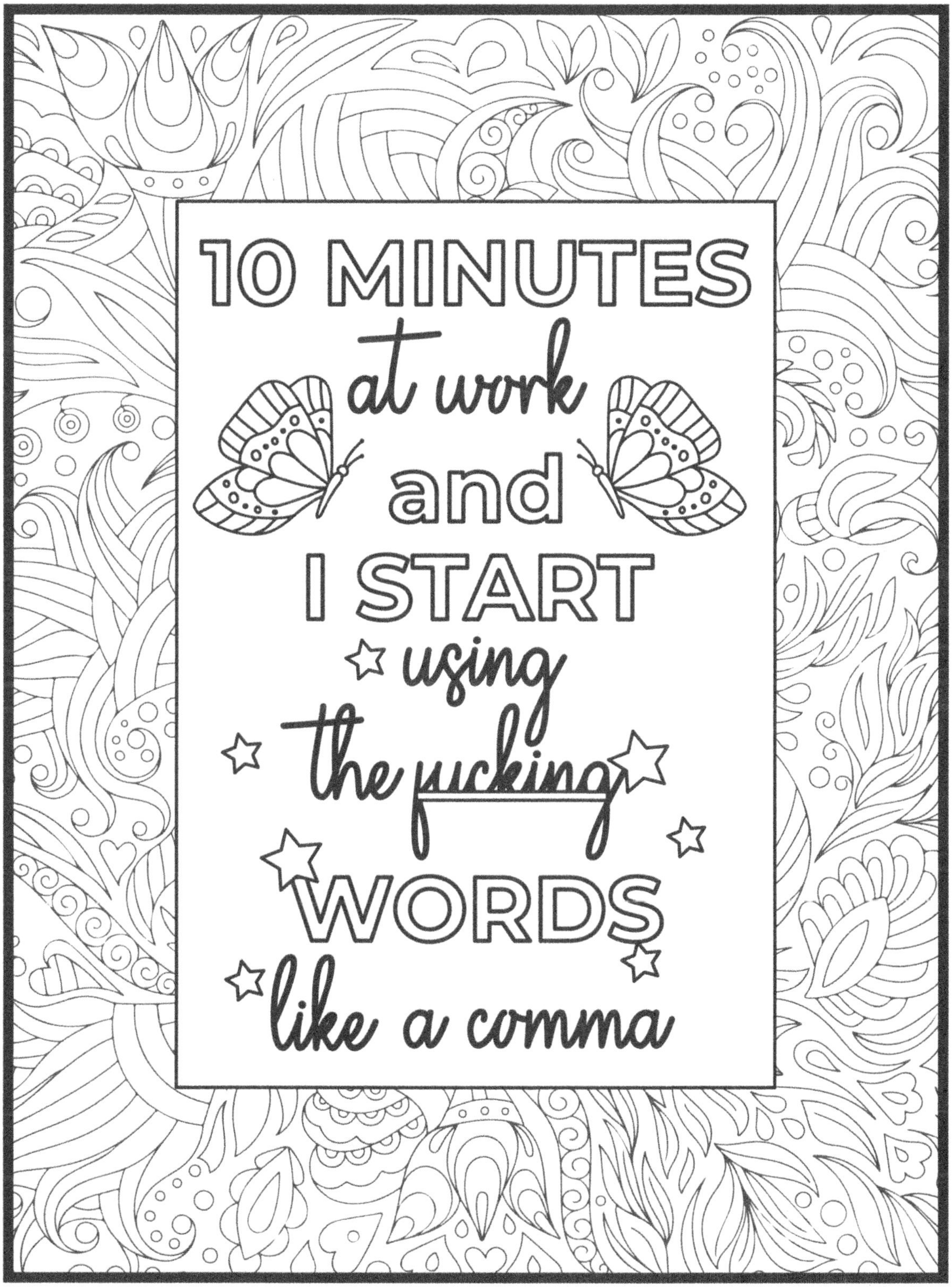
10 MINUTES
at work
and
I START
using
the fucking
WORDS
like a comma

CALM
THE
FUCK
DOWN

EXCUSE ME WHICH LEVEL OF HELL IS THIS?

WHO LEFT
THE BAG
OF IDIOTS
OPEN?

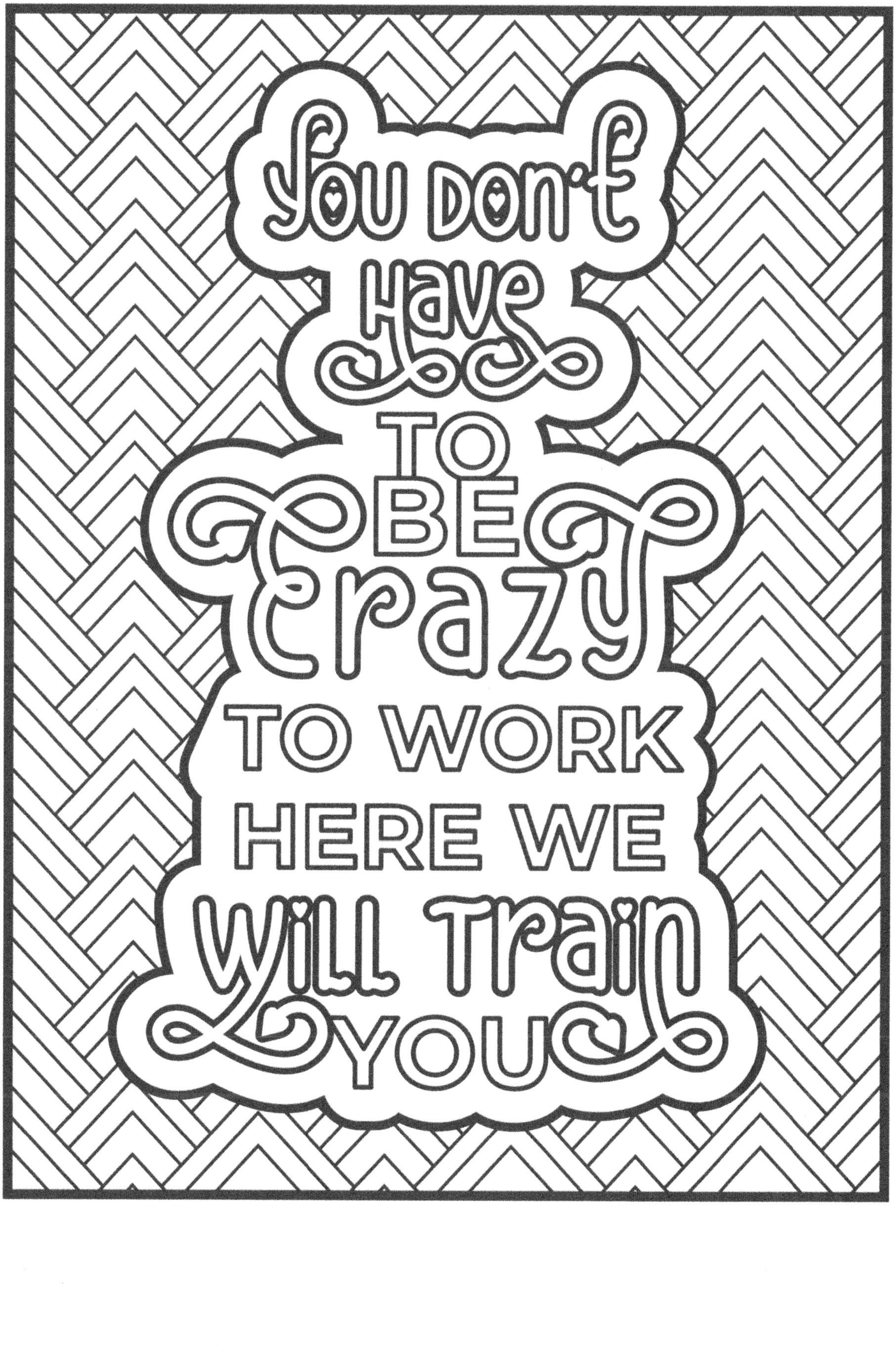
You don't
Have
to
Be
Crazy
TO WORK
HERE WE
Will Train
YOU

YEAH,
WHO
NEEDS
FUCK
ING
holidays
anyway

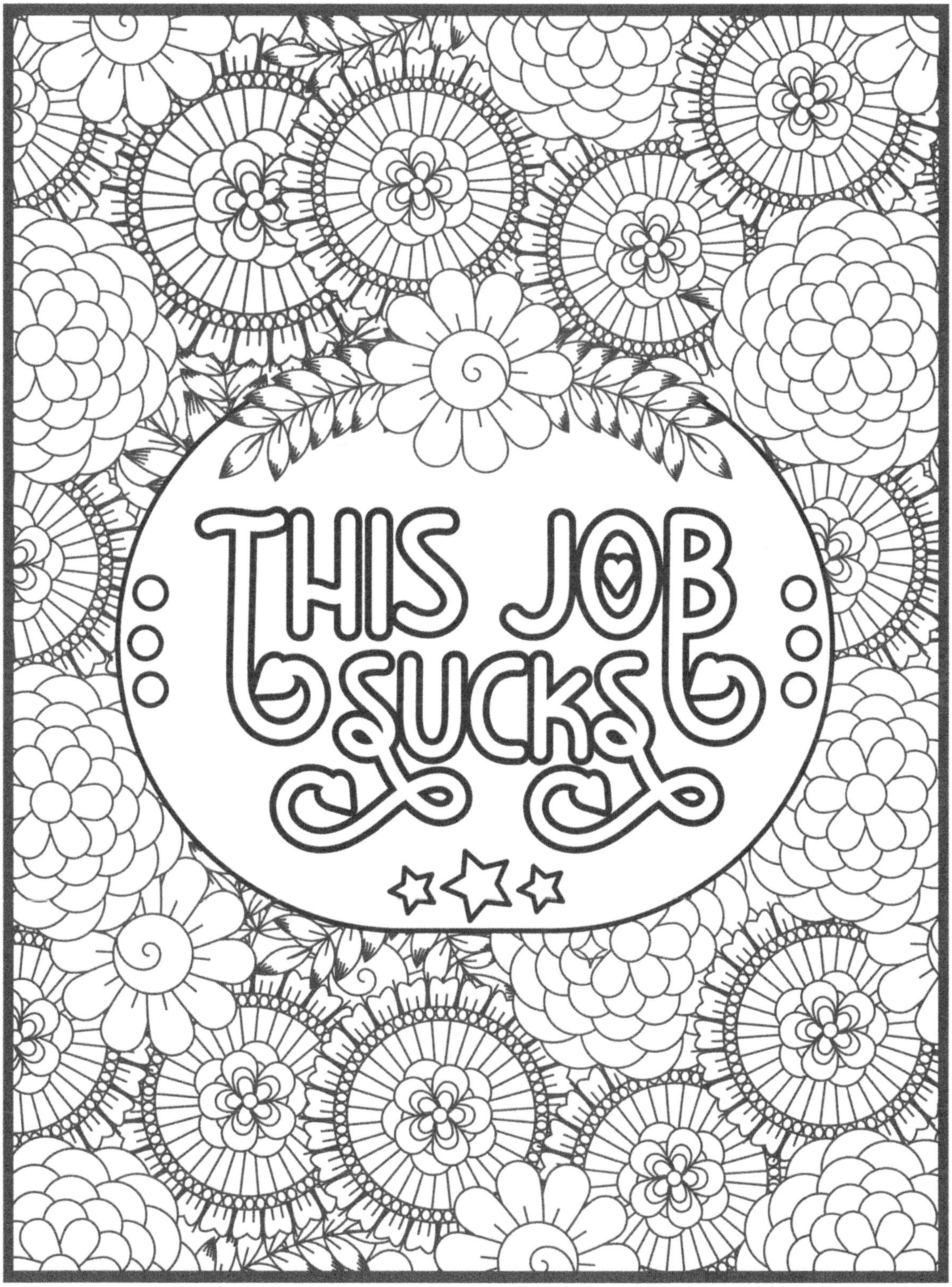
THIS JOB
SUCKS

Made in the USA
Coppell, TX
14 November 2024

40208493R00031